The Case Of Oscar Slater

Sir Arthur Conan Doyle

THE CASE OF
OSCAR SLATER

A. CONAN DOYLE

THE CASE OF
OSCAR SLATER

BY

Sir ARTHUR CONAN DOYLE

AUTHOR OF "THE LOST WORLD," "SHERLOCK HOLMES,"
"THE WHITE COMPANY," ETC.

HODDER & STOUGHTON
NEW YORK
GEORGE H. DORAN COMPANY

THE CASE OF OSCAR SLATER

THE CASE OF OSCAR SLATER

IT is impossible to read and weigh the facts in connection with the conviction of Oscar Slater in May, 1909, at the High Court in Edinburgh, without feeling deeply dissatisfied with the proceedings, and morally certain that justice was not done. Under the circumstances of Scotch law I am not clear how far any remedy exists, but it will, in my opinion, be a serious scandal if the man be allowed upon such evidence to spend his life in a convict prison. The verdict which led to his condemnation to death, was given by a jury of fifteen, who voted: Nine for "Guilty," five for "Non-proven," and one for "Not Guilty." Under English law, this division of opinion would naturally have given cause for a new trial. In Scotland the man was condemned to death, he was only reprieved two days before his execution, and he is now working

7

out a life sentence in Peterhead convict establishment. How far the verdict was a just one, the reader may judge for himself when he has perused a connected story of the case.

There lived in Glasgow in the year 1908, an old maiden lady named Miss Marion Gilchrist. She had lived for thirty years in the one flat, which was on the first floor in 15, Queen's Terrace. The flat above hers was vacant, and the only immediate neighbours were a family named Adams, living on the ground floor below, their house having a separate door which was close alongside the flat entrance. The old lady had one servant, named Helen Lambie, who was a girl twenty-one years of age. This girl had been with Miss Gilchrist for three or four years. By all accounts Miss Gilchrist was a most estimable person, leading a quiet and uneventful life. She was comfortably off, and she had one singular characteristic for a lady of her age and surroundings, in that she had made a collection of jewelry of considerable value. These jewels, which took the form of brooches, rings, pendants, etc., were bought at different times, extending

8

over a considerable number of years, from a reputable jeweller. I lay stress upon the fact, as some wild rumour was circulated at the time that the old lady might herself be a criminal receiver. Such an idea could not be entertained. She seldom wore her jewelry save in single pieces, and as her life was a retired one, it is difficult to see how anyone outside a very small circle could have known of her hoard. The value of this treasure was about three thousand pounds. It was a fearful joy which she snatched from its possession, for she more than once expressed apprehension that she might be attacked and robbed. Her fears had the practical result that she attached two patent locks to her front door, and that she arranged with the Adams family underneath that in case of alarm she would signal to them by knocking upon the floor.

It was the household practice that Lambie, the maid, should go out and get an evening paper for her mistress about seven o'clock each day. After bringing the paper she then usually went out again upon the necessary shopping. This routine was followed upon the night of December 21st. She left her mistress seated by the fire in the dining-room reading a magazine. Lambie took the keys with her, shut the flat door, closed the hall door downstairs, and was gone about ten minutes upon her errand. It is the events of those ten minutes which form the tragedy and the mystery which were so soon to engage the attention of the public.

According to the girl's evidence, it was a minute or two before seven when she went out. At about seven, Mr. Arthur Adams and his two sisters were in their dining-room immediately below the room in which the old lady had been left. Suddenly they heard " a noise from above, then a very heavy fall, and then three sharp knocks." They were alarmed at the sound, and the young man at once set off to see if all was right. He ran out of his hall door, through the hall door of the flats, which was open, and so up to the first floor, where he found Miss Gilchrist's door shut. He rang three times without an answer. From within, however, he heard a sound which he compared to the breaking of sticks. He imagined therefore that the servant girl was within, and that she was engaged in her household duties. After waiting for a minute or two, he seems to have convinced himself that all was right. He therefore descended again and returned to his sisters, who persuaded him to go up once more to the flat. This he did and rang for the fourth time. As he was standing with his hand upon the bell, straining his ears and hearing nothing, someone approached up the stairs from below. It was the young servant-maid, Helen Lambie, returning from her errand. The two held council for a moment. Young Adams described the noise which had been heard. Lambie said that the pulleys of the clothes-lines in the kitchen must have given way. It was a singular explanation, since the kitchen was not above the dining-room of the Adams, and one would not expect any great noise from the fall of a cord which suspended sheets or towels. However, it was a moment of agitation, and the girl may have said the first explanation which came into her head. She then put her keys into the

11

two safety locks and opened the door.

At this point there is a curious little discrepancy of evidence. Lambie is prepared to swear that she remained upon the mat beside young Adams. Adams is equally positive that she walked several paces down the hall. This inside hall was lit by a gas, which turned half up, and shining through a coloured shade, gave a sufficient, but not a brilliant light. Says Adams: "I stood at the door on the threshold, half in and half out, and just when the girl had got past the clock to go into the kitchen, a well-dressed man appeared. I did not suspect him, and she said nothing; and he came up to me quite pleasantly. I did not suspect anything wrong for the minute. I thought the man was going to speak to me, till he got past me, and then I suspected something wrong, and by that time the girl ran into the kitchen and put the gas up and said it was all right, meaning her pulleys. I said: 'Where is your mistress?' and she went into the dining-room. She said: 'Oh! come here!' I just went in and saw this horrible spectacle."

THE CASE OF OSCAR SLATER

The spectacle in question was the poor old lady lying upon the floor close by the chair in which the servant had last seen her. Her feet were towards the door, her head towards the fireplace. She lay upon a hearth-rug, but a skin rug had been thrown across her head. Her injuries were frightful, nearly every bone of her face and skull being smashed. In spite of her dreadful wounds she lingered for a few minutes, but died without showing any sign of consciousness.

The murderer when he had first appeared had emerged from one of the two bedrooms at the back of the hall, the larger, or spare bedroom, not the old lady's room. On passing Adams upon the doormat, which he had done with the utmost coolness, he had at once rushed down the stair. It was a dark and drizzly evening, and it seems that he made his way along one or two quiet streets until he was lost in the more crowded thoroughfares. He had left no weapon nor possession of any sort in the old lady's flat, save a box of matches with which he had lit the gas in the bedroom from which he had come. In this bedroom a number of articles of value, including a watch, lay upon the dressing-table, but none of them had been touched. A box containing papers had been forced open, and these papers were found scattered upon the floor. If he were really in search of the jewels, he was badly informed, for these were kept among the dresses in the old lady's wardrobe. Later, a single crescent diamond brooch, an article worth perhaps forty or fifty pounds, was found to be missing. Nothing else was taken from the flat. It is remarkable that though the furniture round where the body lay was spattered with blood, and one would have imagined that the murderer's hands must have been stained, no mark was seen upon the half-consumed match with which he had lit the gas, nor upon the match box, the box containing papers, nor any other thing which he may have touched in the bedroom.

We come now to the all-important question of the description of the man seen at such close quarters by Adams and Lambie. Adams was short-sighted and had not his spectacles with him. His evidence at the trial ran thus:

"He was a man a little taller and a little broader than I am, not a well-built man but well featured and clean-shaven, and I cannot exactly swear to his moustache, but if he had any it was very little. He was rather a commercial traveller type, or perhaps a clerk, and I did not know but what he might be one of her friends. He had on dark trousers and a light overcoat. I could not say if it were fawn or grey. I do not recollect what sort of hat he had. He seemed gentlemanly and well-dressed. He had nothing in his hand so far as I could tell. I did not notice anything about his way of walking."

Helen Lambie, the other spectator, could give no information about the face (which rather bears out Adams' view as to her position), and could only say that he wore a round cloth hat, a three-quarter length overcoat of a grey colour, and that he had some peculiarity in his walk. As the distance traversed by the murderer within sight of Lambie could be crossed in four steps, and as these steps were taken under circumstances of peculiar agitation, it is difficult to think that any importance could be attached to this last item in the description.

It is impossible to avoid some comment upon the actions of Helen Lambie during the incidents just narrated, which can only be explained by supposing that from the time she saw Adams waiting outside her door, her whole reasoning faculty had deserted her. First, she explained the great noise heard below: "The ceiling was like to crack," said Adams, by the fall of a clothes-line and its pulleys of attachment, which could not possibly, one would imagine, have produced any such effect. She then declares that she remained upon the mat, while Adams is convinced that she went right down the hall. On the appearance of the stranger she did not gasp out: "Who are you?" or any other sign of amazement, but allowed Adams to suppose by her silence that the man might be someone who had a right to be there. Finally, instead of rushing at once to see if her mistress was safe, she went into the kitchen, still apparently under the obsession of the pulleys. She informed Adams that they were all right,

16

as if it mattered to any human being; thence she went into the spare bedroom, where she must have seen that robbery had been committed, since an open box lay in the middle of the floor. She gave no alarm however, and it was only when Adams called out: "Where is your mistress?" that she finally went into the room of the murder. It must be admitted that this seems strange conduct, and only explicable, if it can be said to be explicable, by great want of intelligence and grasp of the situation.

On Tuesday, December 22nd, the morning after the murder, the Glasgow police circulated a description of the murderer, founded upon the joint impressions of Adams and of Lambie. It ran thus:

"A man between 25 and 30 years of age, five foot eight or nine inches in height, slim build, dark hair, clean-shaven, dressed in light grey overcoat and dark cloth cap."

Four days later, however, upon Christmas Day, the police found themselves in a position to give a more detailed description:

"The man wanted is about 28 or 30 years

of age, tall and thin, with his face shaved clear of all hair, while a distinctive feature is that his nose is slightly turned to one side. The witness thinks the twist is to the right side. He wore one of the popular tweed hats known as Donegal hats, and a fawn coloured overcoat which might have been a waterproof, also dark trousers and brown boots."

The material from which these further points were gathered, came from a young girl of fifteen, in humble life, named Mary Barrowman. According to this new evidence, the witness was passing the scene of the murder shortly after seven o'clock upon the fatal night. She saw a man run hurriedly down the steps, and he passed her under a lamp-post. The incandescent light shone clearly upon him. He ran on, knocking against the witness in his haste, and disappeared round a corner. On hearing later of the murder, she connected this incident with it. Her general recollections of the man were as given in the description, and the grey coat and cloth cap of the first two witnesses were given up in favour of the fawn coat and round Donegal hat of the young girl. Since she had seen no peculiarity in his walk, and they had seen none in his nose, there is really nothing the same in the two descriptions save the " clean-shaven," the " slim build " and the approximate age.

It was on the evening of Christmas Day that the police came at last upon a definite clue. It was brought to their notice that a German Jew of the assumed name of Oscar Slater had been endeavouring to dispose of the pawn ticket of a crescent diamond brooch of about the same value as the missing one. Also, that in a general way, he bore a resemblance to the published description. Still more hopeful did this clue appear when, upon raiding the lodgings in which this man and his mistress lived, it was found that they had left Glasgow that very night by the nine o'clock train, with tickets (over this point there was some clash of evidence) either for Liverpool or London. Three days later, the Glasgow police learned that the couple had actually sailed upon December 26th upon the Lusitania for New York under the name of Mr. and Mrs. Otto Sando. It must be admitted that in all these proceedings the Glasgow police showed considerable deliberation. The original information had been given at the Central Police Office shortly after six o'clock, and a detective was actually making enquiries at Slater's flat at seven-thirty, yet no watch was kept upon his movements, and he was allowed to leave between eight and nine, untraced and unquestioned. Even stranger was the Liverpool departure. He was known to have got away in the southbound train upon the Friday evening. A great liner sails from Liverpool upon the Saturday. One would have imagined that early on the Saturday morning steps would have been taken to block his method of escape. However, as a fact, it was not done, and as it proved it is as well for the cause of justice, since it had the effect that two judicial processes were needed, an American and a Scottish, which enables an interesting comparison to be made between the evidence of the principal witnesses.

Oscar Slater was at once arrested upon arriving at New York, and his seven trunks of baggage were impounded and sealed. On the face of it there was a good case against him, for he had undoubtedly pawned a diamond brooch, and he had subsequently fled under a false name for America. The Glasgow police had reason to think that they had got their man. Two officers, accompanied by the witnesses to identity — Adams, Lambie and Barrowman — set off at once to carry through the extradition proceedings and bring the suspect back to be tried for his offence. In the New York Court they first set eyes upon the prisoner, and each of them, in terms which will be afterwards described, expressed the opinion that he was at any rate exceedingly like the person they had seen in Glasgow. Their actual identification of him was vitiated by the fact that Adams and Barrowman had been shown his photographs before attending the Court, and also that he was led past them, an obvious prisoner, whilst they were waiting in the corridor. Still, however much one may discount the actual identification, it cannot be denied that each witness saw a close resemblance between the man before them and the man whom they had seen in Glasgow. So far at every stage the case against the accused. was becoming more menacing. Any doubt as ·to extradition was speedily set at rest by the prisoner's announcement that he was prepared, without compulsion, to return to Scotland and to stand his trial. One may well refuse to give him any excessive credit for this surrender, since he may have been persuaded that things were going against him, but still the fact remains (and it was never, so far as I can trace, mentioned at his subsequent trial), that he gave himself up of his own free will to justice. On February 21st Oscar Slater was back in Glasgow once more, and on May 3rd his trial took place at the High Court in Edinburgh.

But already the very bottom of the case had dropped out. The starting link of what had seemed an imposing chain, had suddenly broken. It will be remembered that the original suspicion of Slater was founded upon the fact that he had pawned a crescent diamond brooch. The ticket was found upon him, and the brooch recovered. It was not the one which was missing from the room of the murdered woman, and it had belonged for years to Slater, who had repeatedly pawned it before. This was shown beyond all cavil or dispute. The case of the police might well seem desperate after this, since if Slater were indeed guilty, it would mean that by pure chance they had pursued the right man. The coincidence involved in such a supposition would seem to pass the limits of all probability.

Apart from this crushing fact, several of the other points of the prosecution had already shown themselves to be worthless. It had seemed at first that Slater's departure had been sudden and unpremeditated — the flight of a guilty man. It was quickly proved that this was not so. In the Bohemian clubs which he frequented — he was by profession a peddling jeweller and a man of disreputable, though not criminal habits — it had for weeks before the date of the crime been known that he purported to go to some business associates in America. A correspondence, which was produced, showed the arrangements which had

23

been made, long before the crime, for his emigration, though it should be added that the actual determination of the date and taking of the ticket were subsequent to the tragedy.

This hurrying-up of the departure certainly deserves close scrutiny. According to the evidence of his mistress and of the servant, Slater had received two letters upon the morning of December 21st. Neither of these were produced at the trial. One was said to be from a Mr. Rogers, a friend of Slater's in London, telling him that Slater's wife was bothering him for money. The second was said to be from one Devoto, a former partner of Slater's asking him to join him in San Francisco. Even if the letters had been destroyed, one would imagine that these statements as to the letters could be disproved or corroborated by either the Crown or the defence. They are of considerable importance, as giving the alleged reasons why Slater hurried up a departure which had been previously announced as for January. I cannot find, however, that in the actual trial anything definite was ascertained upon the matter.

Another point had already been scored against the prosecution in that the seven trunks which contained the whole effects of the prisoner, yielded nothing of real importance. There were a felt hat and two cloth ones, but none which correspond with the Donegal of the original description. A light-coloured waterproof coat was among the outfit. If the weapon with which the deed was done was carried off in the pocket of the assassin's overcoat — and it is difficult to say how else he could have carried it, then the pocket must, one would suppose, be crusted with blood, since the crime was a most sanguinary one. No such marks were discovered, nor were the police fortunate as to the weapon. It is true that a hammer was found in the trunk, but it was clearly shown to have been purchased in one of those cheap half-crown sets of tools which are tied upon a card, was an extremely light and fragile instrument, and utterly incapable in the eyes of commonsense of inflicting those terrific injuries which had shattered the old lady's skull. It is said by the prosecution to bear some marks of having been scraped or cleaned, but this was vigorously denied by the defence, and the police do not appear to have pushed the matter to the obvious test of removing the metal work, when they must, had this been indeed the weapon, have certainly found some soakage of blood into the wood under the edges of the iron cheeks or head. But a glance at a facsimile of this puny weapon would convince an impartial person that any task beyond fixing a tin-tack, or cracking a small bit of coal, would be above its strength. It may fairly be said that before the trial had begun, the three important points of the pawned jewel, the supposed flight, and the evidence from clothing and weapon, had each either broken down completely, or become exceedingly attenuated.

Let us see now what there was upon the other side. The evidence for the prosecution really resolved itself into two sets of witnesses for identification. The first set were those who had actually seen the murderer, and included Adams, Helen Lambie, and the girl Barrowman. The second set consisted of

26

twelve people who had, at various dates, seen a man frequenting the street in which Miss Gilchrist lived, and loitering in a suspicious manner before the house. All of these, some with confidence, but most of them with reserve, were prepared to identify the prisoner with this unknown man. What the police never could produce, however, was the essential thing, and that was the least connecting link between Slater and Miss Gilchrist, or any explanation how a foreigner in Glasgow could even know of the existence, to say nothing of the wealth, of a retired old lady, who had few acquaintances and seldom left her guarded flat.

It is notorious that nothing is more tricky than evidence of identification. In the Beck case there were, if I remember right, some ten witnesses who had seen the real criminal under normal circumstances, and yet they were all prepared to swear to the wrong man. In the case of Oscar Slater, the first three witnesses saw their man under conditions of excitement, while the second group saw the loiterer in the street under various lights, and in a fashion which was always more or less casual. It is right, therefore, that in assigning its due weight to this evidence, one should examine it with some care. We shall first take the three people who actually saw the murderer.

There seems to have been some discrepancy between them from the first, since, as has already been pointed out, the description published from the data of Adams and Lambie, was modified after Barrowman had given her information. Adams and Lambie said:

"A man between twenty-five and thirty years of age, 5 feet 8 or 9 inches in height, slim build, dark hair, clean shaven, dressed in light grey overcoat and dark cloth cap."

After collaboration with Barrowman the description became:

"Twenty-eight or thirty years of age, tall and thin, clean shaven, his nose slightly turned to one side. Wore one of the popular round tweed hats known as Donegal hats, and a fawn-coloured overcoat which might have been a waterproof, also dark trousers and brown boots."

Apart from the additions in the second description there are, it will be observed, two actual discrepancies in the shape of the hat and the colour of the coat.

As to how far either of these descriptions tallies with Slater, it may be stated here that the accused was thirty-seven years of age, that he was above the medium height, that his nose was not twisted, but was depressed at the end, as if it had at some time been broken, and finally that eight witnesses were called upon to prove that, on the date of the murder, the accused wore a short but noticeable moustache.

I have before me a verbatim stenographic report of the proceedings in New York and also in Edinburgh, furnished by the kindness of Shaughnessy & Co., solicitors, of Glasgow, who are still contending for the interests of their unfortunate client. I will here compare the terms of the identification in the two Courts:

Helen Lambie, New York, January 26th, 1909.

Q. "Do you see the man here you saw there?"

A. "One is very suspicious, if anything."

Q. "Describe him."

A. "The clothes he had on that night he hasn't got on to-day — but his face I could not tell. I never saw his face."

(Having described a peculiarity of walk, she was asked):

Q. "Is that man in the room?"

A. "Yes, he is, sir."

Q. "Point him out."

A. "I would not like to say ——"

(After some pressure and argument she pointed to Slater, who had been led past her in the corridor between two officers, when both she and Barrowman had exclaimed: "That is the man," or "I could nearly swear that is the man.")

Q. "Didn't you say you did not see the man's face?"

A. "Neither I did. I saw the walk."

The reader must bear in mind that Lambie's only chance of seeing the man's walk was in the four steps or so down the passage. It was never at any time shown that there was any marked peculiarity about Slater's walk.

Now take Helen Lambie's identification in Edinburgh, May 9th, 1909.

Q. "How did you identify him in America?"

A. "By his walk and height, his dark hair and the side of his face."

Q. "You were not quite sure of him at first in America?"

A. "Yes, I was quite sure."

Q. "Why did you say you were only suspicions?"

A. "It was a mistake."

Q. "What did you mean in America by saying that you never saw his face if, in point of fact, you did see it so as to help you to recognise it? What did you mean?"

A. "Nothing."

On further cross-examination she declared that when she said that she had never seen the man's face she meant that she had never seen the "broad of it" but had seen it sideways.

Here it will be observed that Helen Lambie's evidence had greatly stiffened during the three months between the New York and the

Edinburgh proceedings. In so aggressively positive a frame of mind was she on the later occasion, that, on being shown Slater's overcoat and asked if it resembled the murderer's, she answered twice over: " That is the coat," although it had not yet been unrolled, and though it was not light grey, which was the colour in her own original description. It should not be forgotten in dealing with the evidence of Lambie and Adams that they are utterly disagreed as to so easily fixed a thing as their own proceedings after the hall door was opened, Adams swearing that Lambie walked to nearly the end of the hall, and Lambie that she remained upon the doormat. Without deciding which was right, it is clear that the incident must shake one's confidence in one or other of them as a witness.

In the case of Adams the evidence was given with moderation, and was substantially the same in America and in Scotland.

" I couldn't say positively. This man (indicating Slater) is not at all unlike him."

Q. " Did you notice a crooked nose? "

A. " No."

Q. "Anything remarkable about his walk?"

A. "No."

Q. "You don't swear this is the man you saw?"

A. "No, sir. He resembles the man, that is all that I can say."

In reply to the same general questions in Edinburgh, he said:

"I would not like to swear he is the man. I am a little near-sighted. He resembles the man closely."

Barrowman, the girl of fifteen, had met the man presumed to be the murderer in the street, and taken one passing glance at him under a gas lamp on a wet December's night — difficult circumstances for an identification. She used these words in New York:

"That man here is something like him," which she afterwards amended to "very like him." She admitted that a picture of the man she was expected to identify had been shown to her before she came into the Court. Her one point by which she claimed to recognise the man was the crooked nose. This crooked nose was not much more apparent to others than the peculiarity of walk which so greatly impressed Helen Lambie that, after seeing half a dozen steps of it, she could identify it with confidence. In Edinburgh Barrowman, like Lambie, was very much more certain than in New York. The further they got from the event, the easier apparently did recognition become. "Yes, that is the man who knocked against me that night," she said. It is remarkable that both these females, Lambie and Barrowman, swore that though they were thrown together in this journey out to New York, and actually shared the same cabin, they never once talked of the object of their mission or compared notes as to the man they were about to identify. For girls of the respective ages of fifteen and twenty-one this certainly furnishes a unique example of self-restraint.

These, then, are the three identifications by the only people who saw the murderer. Had the diamond brooch clue been authentic, and these identifications come upon the top of it, they would undoubtedly have been strongly corroborative.   But when the brooch has been shown to be a complete mistake, I really do not understand how anyone could accept such half-hearted recognitions as being enough to establish the identity and guilt of the prisoner.

There remains the so-called identification by twelve witnesses who had seen a man loitering in the street during the weeks before the crime had been committed. I have said a "so-called" identification, for the proceedings were farcical as a real test of recognition. The witnesses had seen portraits of the accused. They were well aware that he was a foreigner, and then they were asked to pick out his swarthy Jewish physiognomy from among nine Glasgow policemen to two railway officials. Naturally they did it without hesitation, since this man was more like the dark individual whom they had seen and described than the others could be.

Read their own descriptions, however, of the man they had seen, with the details of his clothing, and they will be found in many respects to differ from each other on one hand,

and in many from Slater on the other. Here is a synopsis of their impressions:

Mrs. McHaffie.—" Dark. Moustached, light overcoat, not waterproof, check trousers, spats. Black bowler hat. Nose normal."

Miss M. McHaffie.— " Seen at same time and same description. Was only prepared at first to say there was some resemblance, but ' had been thinking it over, and concluded that he was the man.' "

Miss A. M. McHaffie.— " Same as before. Had heard the man speak and noticed nothing in his accent. (Prisoner has a strong German accent.) "

Madge McHaffie (belongs to the same family).— " Dark, moustached, nose normal. Check trousers, fawn overcoat and spats. Black bowler hat. ' The prisoner was fairly like the man .' "

In connection with the identification of these four witnesses it is to be observed that neither check trousers, nor spats were found in the prisoner's luggage. As the murderer was described as being dressed in dark trousers, there was no possible reason why these clothes, if

Slater owned them, should have been destroyed.

Constable Brien. "Claimed to know the prisoner by sight. Says he was the man he saw loitering. Light coat and a hat. It was a week before the crime, and he was loitering eighty yards from the scene of it. He picked him out among five constables as the man he had seen."

Constable Walker.— "Had seen the loiterer across the street, never nearer, and after dark in December. Thought at first he was someone else whom he knew. Had heard that the man he had to identify was of foreign appearance. Picked him out from a number of detectives. The man seen had a moustache."

Euphemia Cunningham.— "Very dark, sallow, heavy featured. Clean shaven. Nose normal. Dark tweed coat. Green cap with peak."

W. Campbell.— "Had been with the previous witness. Corroborated. 'There was a general resemblance between the prisoner and the man, but he could not positively identify him.'"

Alex Gillies.—"Sallow, dark haired and clean shaven. Fawn coat. Cap. 'The prisoner resembled him, but witness could not say he was the same man.'"

R. B. Bryson.—"Black coat and vest. Black bowler hat. No overcoat. Black moustache with droop. Sallow, foreign. (This witness had seen the man the night before the murder. He appeared to be looking up at Miss Gilchrist's windows.)"

A. Nairn.—"Broad shoulders, long neck. Dark hair. Motor cap. Light overcoat to knees. Never saw the man's face. 'Oh! I will not swear in fact, but I am certain he is the man I saw — but I will not swear.'"

Mrs. Liddell.—"Peculiar nose. Clear complexion, not sallow. Dark, clean shaven, brown tweed cap. Brown tweed coat with hemmed edge. Delicate man 'rather drawn together.' She believed that prisoner was the man. Saw him in the street immediately before the murder."

These are the twelve witnesses as to the identify of the mysterious stranger. In the first place there is no evidence whatever that this lounger in the street had really anything to do with the murder. It is just as probable that he had some vulgar amour, and was waiting for his girl to run out to him. What could a man who was planning murder hope to gain by standing nights beforehand eighty and a hundred yards away from the place in the darkness? But supposing that we waive this point and examine the plain question as to whether Slater was the same man as the loiterer, we find ourselves faced by a mass of difficulties and contradictions. Two of the most precise witnesses were Nairn and Bryson who saw the stranger upon the Sunday night preceding the murder. Upon that night Slater had an unshaken alibi, vouched for not only by the girl, Antoine, with whom he lived, and their servant, Schmalz, but by an acquaintance, Samuel Reid, who had been with him from six to ten-thirty. This positive evidence, which was quite unshaken in cross examination, must completely destroy the surmises of the stranger and Slater. Then come the four witnesses of the McHaffie family who are all strong upon check trousers and spats, articles of dress which were never traced to the prisoner. Finally, apart from the discrepancies about the moustache, there is a mixture of bowler hats, green caps, brown caps, and motor caps which leave a most confused and indefinite impression in the mind. Evidence of this kind might be of some value if supplementary to some strong ascertained fact, but to attempt to build upon such an identification alone is to construct the whole case upon shifting sand.

The reader has already a grasp of the facts, but some fresh details came out at the trial which may be enumerated here. They have to be lightly touched upon within the limits of such an argument as this, but those who desire a fuller summary will find it in an account of the trial published by Hodge of Edinburgh, and ably edited by William Roughead, W.S. On this book and on the verbatim precognitions and shorthand account of the American proceedings, I base my own examination of case. First, as to Slater's movements upon the day of the crime. He began the day, according to the account of himself and the women, by the receipt of the two letters already referred to, which caused him to hasten his journey to America. The whole day seems to have been occupied by preparations for his impending departure. He gave his servant Schmalz notice as from next Saturday. Before five (as was shown by the postmark upon the envelope), he wrote to a post office in London, where he had some money on deposit. At 6.12 a telegram was sent in his name and presumably by him from the Central Station to Dent, London, for his watch, which was being repaired. According to the evidence of two witnesses he was seen in a billiard room at 6.20. The murder, it will be remembered, was done at seven. He remained about ten minutes in the billiard room, and left some time between 6.30 and 6.40. Rathman, one of these witnesses, deposed that he had at the time a moustache about a quarter of an inch long, which was so noticeable that no one could take him for a clean-shaven man. Antoine, his mistress, and Schmalz, the servant, both deposed that Slater dined at home at 7 o'clock. The evidence of the girl

41

is no doubt suspect, but there was no possible reason why the dismissed servant Schmalz should perjure herself for the sake of her ex-employer. The distance between Slater's flat and that of Miss Gilchrist is about a quarter of a mile. From the billiard room to Slater's flat is about a mile. He had to go for the hammer and bring it back, unless he had it jutting out of his pocket all day. But unless the evidence of the two women is entirely set aside, enough has been said to show that there was no time for the commission by him of such a crime and the hiding of the traces which it would leave behind it. At 9.45 that night, Slater was engaged in his usual occupation of trying to raise the wind at some small gambling club. The club-master saw no discomposure about his dress (which was the same as, according to the Crown, he had done this bloody crime in), and swore that he was then wearing a short moustache "like stubble," thus corroborating Rathman. It will be remembered that Lambie and Barrowman both swore that the murderer was clean shaven.

On December 24th, three days after the murder, Slater was shown at Cook's Office, bargaining for a berth in the "Lusitania" for his so-called wife and himself. He made no secret that he was going by that ship, but gave his real name and address and declared finally that he would take his berth in Liverpool, which he did. Among other confidants as to the ship was a barber, the last person one would think to whom secrets would be confided. Certainly, if this were a flight, it is hard to say what an open departure would be. In Liverpool he took his passage under the assumed name of Otto Sando. This he did, according to his own account, because he had reason to fear pursuit from his real wife, and wished to cover his traces. This may or may not be the truth, but it is undoubtedly the fact that Slater, who was a disreputable, rolling-stone of a man, had already assumed several aliases in the course of his career. It is to be noted that there was nothing at all secret about his departure from Glasgow, and that he carried off all his luggage with him in a perfectly open manner.

The reader is now in possession of the main

facts, save those which are either unessential, or redundant. It will be observed that save for the identifications, the value of which can be estimated, there is really no single point of connection between the crime and the alleged criminal. It may be argued that the existence of the hammer is such a point; but what household in the land is devoid of a hammer? It is to be remembered that if Slater committed the murder with this hammer, he must have taken it with him in order to commit the crime, since it could be no use to him in forcing an entrance. But what man in his senses, planning a deliberate murder, would take with him a weapon which was light, frail, and so long that it must project from any pocket? The nearest lump of stone upon the road would serve his purpose better than that. Again, it must in its blood-soaked condition have been in his pocket when he came away from the crime. The Crown never attempted to prove either blood-stains in a pocket, or the fact that any clothes had been burned. If Slater destroyed clothes, he would naturally have destroyed the hammer, too. Even one of the two medical witnesses of the prosecution was driven to say that he should not have expected such a weapon to cause such wounds.

It may well be that in this summary of the evidence, I may seem to have stated the case entirely from the point of view of the defence. In reply, I would only ask the reader to take the trouble to read the extended evidence. ("Trial of Oscar Slater" Hodge & Co., Edinburgh.) If he will do so, he will realise that without a conscious mental effort towards special pleading, there is no other way in which the story can be told. The facts are on one side. The conjectures, the unsatisfactory identifications, the damaging flaws, and the very strong prejudices upon the other.

Now for the trial itself. The case was opened for the Crown by the Lord-Advocate, in a speech which faithfully represented the excited feeling of the time. It was vigorous to the point of being passionate, and its effect upon the jury was reflected in their ultimate verdict. The Lord-Advocate spoke, as I understand, without notes, a procedure which may well add to eloquence while subtracting

45

from accuracy. It is to this fact that one must attribute a most fatal mis-statement which could not fail, coming under such circumstances from so high an authority, to make a deep impression upon his hearers. For some reason, this mis-statement does not appear to have been corrected at the moment by either the Judge or the defending counsel. It was the one really damaging allegation — so damaging that had I myself been upon the jury and believed it to be true, I should have recorded my verdict against the prisoner, and yet this one fatal point had no substance at all in fact. In this incident alone, there seems to me to lie good ground for a revision of the sentence, or a reference of the facts to some Court or Committee of Appeal. Here is the extract from the Lord-Advocate's speech to which I allude:

"At this time he had given his name to Cook's people in Glasgow as Oscar Slater. On December 25th, the day he was to go back to Cook's Office — his name and his description and all the rest of it appear in the Glasgow papers, and he sees that the last thing in the world that he ought to do, if he studies his own safety, is to go back to Cook's Office as Oscar Slater. He accordingly proceeds to pack up all his goods and effects upon the 25th. So far as we know, he never leaves the house from the time he sees the paper, until a little after six o'clock, when he goes down to the Central Station."

Here the allegation is clearly made and it is repeated later that Oscar Slater's name was in the paper, and that, subsequently to that, he fled. Such a flight would clearly be an admission of guilt. The point is of enormous even vital importance. And yet on examination of the dates, it will be found that there is absolutely no foundation for it. It was not until the evening of the 25th that even the police heard of the existence of Slater, and it was nearly a week later that his name appeared in the papers, he being already far out upon the Atlantic. What did appear upon the 25th was the description of the murderer, already quoted: "with his face shaved clean of all hair," &c., Slater at that time having a marked moustache. Why should he take such a description to himself, or why should he forbear to carry out a journey which he had already prepared for? The point goes for absolutely nothing when examined, and yet if the minds of the jury were at all befogged as to the dates, the definite assertion of the Lord-Advocate, twice repeated, that Slater's name had been published before his flight, was bound to have a most grave and prejudiced effect.

Some of the Lord-Advocate's other statements are certainly surprising. Thus he says: "The prisoner is hopelessly unable to produce a single witness who says that he was anywhere else than at the scene of the murder that night." Let us test this assertion. Here is the evidence of Schmalz, the servant, verbatim. I may repeat that this woman was under no known obligations to Slater and had just received notice from him. The evidence of the mistress that Slater dined in the flat at seven on the night of the murder I pass, but I do not understand why Schmalz's positive corroboration should be treated by the Lord-Advocate as non-existent. The prisoner might well be "hopeless" if his witnesses were to be treated so. Could anything be more positive than this?

Q. "Did he usually come home to dinner?"

A. "Yes, always. Seven o'clock was the usual hour."

Q. "Was it sometimes nearly eight?

A. "It was my fault. Mr. Slater was in."

Q. "But owing to your fault was it about eight before it was served?"

A. "No. Mr. Slater was in after seven, and was waiting for dinner."

This seems very definite. The murder was committed about seven. The murderer may have regained the street about ten minutes or quarter past seven. It was some distance to Slater's flat. If he had done the murder he could hardly have reached it before half-past seven at the earliest. Yet Schmalz says he was in at seven, and so does Antoine. The evidence of the woman may be good or bad, but it is difficult to understand how anyone could state that the prisoner was "hopelessly unable to produce, etc." What evidence could he give, save that of everyone who lived with him?

For the rest, the Lord-Advocate had an easy task in showing that Slater was a worthless fellow, that he lived with and possibly on a woman of easy virtue, that he had several times changed his name, and that generally he was an unsatisfactory Bohemian. No actual criminal record was shown against him. Early in his speech, the Lord-Advocate remarked that he would show later how Slater may have come to know that Miss Gilchrist owned the jewels. No further reference appears to have been made to the matter, and his promise was therefore never fulfilled, though it is clearly of the utmost importance. Later, he stated that from the appearance of the wounds, they Must have been done by a small hammer. There is no " must " in the matter, for it is clear that many other weapons, a burglar's jemmy, for example, would have produced the same effect. He then makes the good point that the prisoner dealt in precious stones, and could therefore dispose of the proceeds of such a robbery. The criminal, he added, was clearly someone who had no acquaintance with the inside of the house, and did not know where the jewels were kept. "That answers to the prisoner." It also, of course, answers to practically every man in Scotland. The Lord-Advocate then gave a summary of the evidence as to the man seen by various witnesses in the street. "Gentlemen, if that was the prisoner, how do you account for his presence there?" Of course, the whole point lies in the italicised phrase. There was, it must be admitted, a consensus of opinion among the witnesses that the prisoner was the man. But what was it compared to the consensus of opinion which wrongfully condemned Beck to penal servitude? The counsel laid considerable stress upon the fact that Mrs. Liddell (one of the Adams family) had seen a man only a few minutes before the murder, loitering in the street, and identified him as Slater. The dress of the man seen in the street was very different from that given as the murderer's. He had a heavy tweed mixture coat of a brownish hue, and a brown peaked cap. The orig-

inal identification by Mrs. Liddell was conveyed in the words: "One, slightly," when she
was asked if any of a group at the police station resembled the man she had seen. Afterwards, like every other female witness, she
became more positive. She declared that she
had the clearest recollection of the man's face,
and yet refused to commit herself as to
whether he was shaven or moustached.

We have then the recognitions of Lambie,
Adams and Barrowman, with their limitations
and developments, which have been already
discussed. Then comes the question of the
so-called "flight" and the change of name
upon the steamer. Had the prisoner been a
man who had never before changed his name,
this incident would be more striking. But
the short glimpse we obtain of his previous
life show several changes of name, and it has
not been suggested that each of them was the
consequence of a crime. He seems to have
been in debt in Glasgow and he also appears
to have had reasons for getting away from the
pursuit of an ill-used wife. The Lord-Advocate said that the change of name "could not

be explained consistently with innocence." That may be true enough, but the change can surely be explained on some cause less grave than murder. Finally, after showing very truly that Slater was a great liar and that not a word he said need be believed unless there were corroboration, the Lord-Advocate wound up with the words: " My submission to you is that this guilt has been brought fairly home to him, that no shadow of doubt exists, that there is no reasonable doubt that he was the perpetrator of this foul murder." The verdict showed that the jury, under the spell of the Lord-Advocate's eloquence, shared this view, but, viewing it in colder blood, it is difficult to see upon what grounds he made so confident an assertion.

Mr. M'Clure, who conducted the defence, spoke truly when, in opening his speech, he declared that " he had to fight a most unfair fight against public prejudice, roused with a fury I do not remember to have seen in any other case." Still he fought this fight bravely and with scrupulous moderation. His appeals were all to reason and never to emotion. He showed how clearly the prisoner had expressed his intention of going to America, weeks before the murder, and how every preparation had been made. On the day after the murder he had told witnesses that he was going to America and had discussed the advantages of various lines, finally telling one of them the particular boat in which he did eventually travel, curious proceedings for a fugitive from justice. Mr. M'Clure described the movements of the prisoner on the night of the murder, after the crime had been committed, showing that he was wearing the very clothes in which the theory of the prosecution made him do the deed, as if such a deed could be done without leaving its traces. He showed incidentally (it is a small point, but a human one) that one of the last actions of Slater in Glasgow was to take great trouble to get an English five-pound note in order to send it as a Christmas present to his parents in Germany. A man who could do this was not all bad. Finally, Mr. M'Clure exposed very clearly the many discrepancies as to identification and warned the jury solemnly as to the dangers which have been so often proved to lurk in this class of evidence. Altogether, it was a broad, comprehensive reply, though where so many points were involved, it is natural that some few may have been overlooked. One does not, for example, find the counsel as insistent as one might expect upon such points as, the failure of the Crown to show how Slater could have known anything at all about the existence of Miss Gilchrist and her jewels, how he got into the flat, and what became of the brooch which, according to their theory, he had carried off. It is ungracious to suggest any additions to so earnest a defence, and no doubt one who is dependent upon printed accounts of the matter may miss points which were actually made, but not placed upon record.

Only on one point must Mr. M'Clure's judgment be questioned, and that is on the most difficult one, which a criminal counsel has ever to decide. He did not place his man in the box. This should very properly be taken as a sign of weakness. I have no means of saying what considerations led Mr. M'Clure to this determination. It certainly told against his client. In the masterly memorial for reprieve drawn up by Slater's solicitor, the late Mr. Spiers, it is stated with the full inner knowledge which that solicitor had, that Slater was all along anxious to give evidence on his own behalf. " He was advised by his counsel not to do so, but not from any knowledge of guilt. He had undergone the strain of a four days' trial. He speaks rather broken English, although quite intelligible — with a foreign accent, and be had been in custody since January." It must be admitted that these reasons are very unconvincing. It is much more probable that the counsel decided that the purely negative evidence which his client could give upon the crime would be dearly paid for by the long recital of sordid amours and blackguard experiences which would be drawn from him on cross-examination and have the most damning effect upon the minds of a respectable Edinburgh jury. And yet, perhaps, counsel did not sufficiently consider the prejudice which is excited — and rightly excited — against the prisoner who shuns the box. Some of this prejudice might have been removed if it had been made more clear that Slater had volunteered to come over and stand his trial of his own free will, without waiting for the verdict of the extradition proceedings.

There remains the summing up of Lord Guthrie. His Lordship threw out the surmise that the assassin may well have gone to the flat without any intention of murder. This is certainly possible, but in the highest degree improbable. He commented with great severity upon Slater's general character. In his summing-up of the case, he recapitulated the familiar facts in an impartial fashion, concluding with the words, " I suppose that you all think that the prisoner possibly is the murderer. You may very likely all think that he probably is the murderer. That, however, will not entitle you to convict him. The Crown have undertaken to prove that he is the murderer. That is the question you have to consider. If you think there is no reasonable doubt about it, you will convict him; if you think there is, you will acquit him."

In an hour and ten minutes the jury had

made up their mind. By a majority they found the prisoner guilty. Out of fifteen, nine, as was afterwards shown, were for guilty, five for non-proven, and one for not guilty. By English law, a new trial would have been needed, ending, possibly, as in the Gardiner case, in the complete acquittal of the prisoner. By Scotch law the majority verdict held good.

"I know nothing about the affair, absolutely nothing," cried the prisoner in a frenzy of despair. "I never heard the name. I know nothing about the affair. I do not know how I could be connected with the affair. I know nothing about it. I came from America on my own account. I can say no more."

Sentence of death was then passed.

The verdict was, it is said, a complete surprise to most of those in the Court, and certainly is surprising when examined after the event. I do not see how any reasonable man can carefully weigh the evidence and not admit that when the unfortunate prisoner cried, "I know nothing about it," he was possibly, and even probably, speaking the literal truth.

Consider the monstrous coincidence which is involved in his guilt, the coincidence that the police owing to their mistake over the brooch, by pure chance started out in pursuit of the right man. Which is A Priori the more probable: That such an unheard-of million-to-one coincidence should have occurred, Or, that the police, having committed themselves to the theory that he was the murderer, refused to admit that they were wrong when the bottom fell out of the original case, and persevered in the hope that vague identifications of a queer-looking foreigner would justify their original action? Outside these identifications, I must repeat once again there is nothing to couple Slater with the murder, or to show that he ever knew, or could have known that such a person as Miss Gilchrist existed.

The admirable memorial for a reprieve drawn up by the solicitors for the defence, and reproduced at the end of this pamphlet, was signed by 20,000 members of the public, and had the effect of changing the death sentence to one of penal servitude for life. The sentence was passed on May 6th. For twenty days the man was left in doubt, and the written reprieve only arrived on May 26th within twenty-four hours of the time for the execution. On July 8th Slater was conveyed to the Peterhead Convict prison. There he has now been for three years, and there he still remains.

I cannot help in my own mind comparing the case of Oscar Slater with another, which I had occasion to examine — that of George Edalji. I must admit that they are not of the same class. George Edalji was a youth of exemplary character. Oscar Slater was .a blackguard. George Edalji was physically incapable of the crime for which he suffered three years' imprisonment (years for which he has not received, after his innocence was established, one shilling of compensation from the nation). Oscar Slater might conceivably have committed the murder, but the balance of proof and probability seems entirely against it. Thus, one cannot feel the same burning sense of injustice over the matter. And yet I trust for the sake of our character not only for justice, but for intelligence, that the judgment may in some way be reconsidered and the man's present punishment allowed to atone for those irregularities of life which helped to make his conviction possible.

Before leaving the case it is interesting to see how far this curious crime may be reconstructed and whether any possible light can be thrown upon it. Using second-hand material one cannot hope to do more than indicate certain possibilities which may already have been considered and tested by the police. The trouble, however, with all police prosecutions is that, having once got what they imagine to be their man, they are not very open to any line of investigation which might lead to other conclusions. Everything which will not fit into the official theory is liable to be excluded. One might make a few isolated comments on the case which may at least give rise to some interesting trains of thought.

One question which has to be asked was whether the assassin was after the jewels at all. It might be urged that the type of man described by the spectators was by no means that of the ordinary thief. When he reached the bedroom and lit the gas, he did not at once seize the watch and rings which were lying openly exposed upon the dressing-table. He did not pick up a half-sovereign which was lying on the dining-room table. His attention was given to a wooden box, the lid of which he wrenched open. (This, I think, was " the breaking of sticks " heard by Adams.) The papers in it were strewed on the ground. Were the papers his object, and the final abstraction of one diamond brooch a mere blind? Personally, I can only point out the possibility of such a solution. On the other hand, it might be urged, if the thief's action seems inconsequential, that Adams had rung and that he already found himself in a desperate situation. It might be said also that save a will it would be difficult to imagine any paper which would account for such an enterprise, while the jewels, on the other hand, were an obvious mark for whoever knew of their existence.

Presuming that the assassin was indeed after the jewels, it is very instructive to note his knowledge of their location, and also its limitations. Why did he go straight into the spare bedroom where the jewels were actually kept? The same question may be asked with equal force if we consider that he was after the papers. Why the spare bedroom? Any knowledge gathered from outside (by a watcher in the back-yard for example) would go to the length of ascertaining which was the old lady's room. One would expect a robber who had gained his information thus, to go straight to that chamber. But this man did not do so. He went straight to the unlikely room in which both jewels and papers actually were. Is not this remarkably suggestive? Does it not pre-suppose a previous acquaintance with the inside of the flat and the ways of its owner?

But now note the limitations of the knowledge. If it were the jewels he was after, he knew what room they were in, but not in what part of the room. A fuller knowledge would have told him they were kept in the wardrobe. And yet he searched a box. If he was after papers, his information was complete; but if he was indeed after the jewels, then we can say that he had the knowledge of one who is conversant, but not intimately conversant, with the household arrangements. To this we may add that he would seem to have shown ignorance of the habits of the inmates, or he would surely have chosen Lambie's afternoon or evening out for his attempt, and not have done it at a time when the girl was bound to be back within a very few minutes. What men had ever visited the house? The number must have been very limited. What friends? what tradesmen? what plumbers? Who brought back the jewels after they had been stored with the jewellers when the old lady went every year to the country? One is averse to throw out vague suspicions which may give pain to innocent people, and yet it is clear that there are lines of inquiry here which should be followed up, however negative the results.

How did the murderer get in if Lambie is correct in thinking that she shut the doors? I cannot get away from the conclusion that he had duplicate keys. In that case all becomes comprehensible, for the old lady — whose faculties were quite normal — would hear the lock go and would not be alarmed, thinking that Lambie had returned before her time. Thus, she would only know her danger when the murderer rushed into the room, and would hardly have time to rise, receive the first blow, and fall, as she was found, beside the chair, upon which she had been sitting. That is intelligible. But if he had not the keys, consider the difficulties. If the old lady had opened the flat door her body would have been found in the passage. Therefore, the police were driven to the hypothesis that the old lady heard the ring, opened the lower stair door from above (as can be done in all Scotch flats), opened the flat door, never looked over the lighted stair to see who was coming up, but returned to her chair and her magazine, leaving the door open, and a free entrance to the murderer. This is possible, but is it not in the highest degree improbable? Miss Gilchrist was nervous of robbery and would not neglect obvious precautions. The ring came immediately after the maid's departure. She could hardly have thought that it was her returning, the less so as the girl had the keys and would not need to ring. If she went as far as the hall door to open it, she only had to take another step to see who was ascending the stair. Would she not have taken it if it were only to say: " What, have you forgotten your keys? " That a nervous old lady should throw open both doors, never look to see who her visitor was, and return to her dining-room is very hard to believe.

And look at it from the murderer's point of view. He had planned out his proceedings. It is notorious that it is the easiest thing in the world to open the lower door of a Scotch flat. The blade of any penknife will do that. If he was to depend upon ringing to get at his victim, it was evidently better for him to ring at the upper door, as otherwise the chance would seem very great that she would look down, s. him coming up the stair, and shut herself in. On the other hand, if he were at the upper door and she answered it, he had only to push his way in. Therefore, the latter would be his course if he rang at all. And yet the police theory is that though he rang, he rang from below. It is not what he would do, and if he did do it, it would be most unlikely that he would get in. How could he suppose that the old lady would do so incredible a thing as leave her door open and return to her reading? If she waited, she might even up to the last instant have shut the door in his face. If one weighs all these reasons, one can hardly fail, I think, to come to the conclusion that the murderer had keys, and that the old lady never rose from her chair until the last instant, because, hearing the keys in the door, she took it for granted that the maid had come back. But if he had keys, how did he get the mould, and how did he get them made? There is a line of inquiry there. The only conceivable alternatives are, that the murderer was actually concealed in the flat when Lambie came out, and of that there is no evidence whatever, or that the visitor was some one whom the old lady knew, in which case he would naturally have been admitted.

There are still one or two singular points which invite comment. One of these, which I have incidentally mentioned, is that neither the match, the match-box, nor the box opened in the bedroom showed any marks of blood.

Yet the crime had been an extraordinarily bloody one. This is certainly very singular. An explanation given by Dr. Adams who was the first medical man to view the body is worthy of attention. He considered that the wounds might have been inflicted by prods downwards from the leg of a chair, in which case the seat of the chair would preserve the clothes and to some extent the hands of the murderer from bloodstains. The condition of one of the chairs seemed to him to favour this supposition. The explanation is ingenious, but I must confess that I cannot understand how such wounds could be inflicted by such an instrument. There were in particular a number of spindle-shaped cuts with a bridge of skin between them which are very suggestive. My first choice as to the weapon which inflicted these would be a burglar's jemmy, which is bifurcated at one end, while the blow which pushed the poor woman's eye into her brain would represent a thrust from the other end. Failing a jemmy, I should choose a hammer, but a very different one from the toy thing from a half-crown card of tools which was exhibited in Court. Surely commonsense would say that such an instrument could burst an eye-ball, but could not possibly drive it deep into the brain, since the short head could not penetrate nearly so far. The hammer, which I would reconstruct from the injuries would be what they call, I believe, a plasterer's hammer, short in the handle, long and strong in the head, with a broad fork behind. But how such a weapon could be used without the user bearing marks of it, is more than I can say. It has never been explained why a rug was laid over the murdered woman. The murderer, as his conduct before Lambie and Adams showed, was a perfectly cool person. It is at least possible that he used the rug as a shield between him and his victim while he battered her with his weapon. His clothes, if not his hands, would in this way be preserved.

I have said that it is of the first importance to trace who knew of the existence of the jewels, since this might greatly help the solution of the problem. In connection with this there is a passage in Lambie's evidence in

New York which is of some importance. I give it from the stenographer's report, condensing in places:

Q. "Do you know in Glasgow a man named —— ——? "

A. "Yes, sir."

Q. "What is his business?"

A. "A book-maker."

Q. "When did you first meet him?"

A. "At a dance."

Q. "What sort of dance?"

A. "A New Year's dance." (That would be New Year of 1908.)

Q. "When did you meet him after that? "

A. "In the beginning of June."

Q. "Where?"

A. "In Glasgow."

Q. "At a street corner?"

A. "No, he came up to the house at Prince's Street."

Q. "Miss Gilchrist's house?"

A. "Yes, sir."

Q. "That was the first time since the dance?"

A. "Yes, sir."

Q. "Do you deny that you had a meeting with him by a letter received from him at a corner of a street in Glasgow?"

A. "I got a letter." •

Q. "To meet him at a street corner?"

A. "Yes."

Q. "The first meeting after the dance?"

A. "Yes."

Q. "And you met him there?"

A. "Yes."

Q. "And you went out with him?"

A. "No, I did not go out with him."

Q. "You went somewhere with him, didn't you?"

A. "Yes, I made an appointment for Sunday."

Q. "Did you know anything about the man?"

A. "Yes, I did, sir."

Q. "What did you know about him?"

A. "I didn't know much."

Q. "How many times did he visit you at Miss Gilchrist's house?"

A. "Once."

Q. "Quite sure of that?"

A. " Quite sure."

Q. " Didn't he come and take tea with you there in her apartment? "

A. " That was at the Coast."

Q. " Then he came to see you at Miss Gilchrist's summer place? "

A. " Yes."

Q. " How many times? "

A. " Once."

Q. " Did he meet Miss Gilchrist then? "

A. " Yes, sir."

Q. " You introduced him? "

A. " Yes, sir."

Q. " Did she wear this diamond brooch? "

A. " I don't remember."

Q. " When did you next see him? "

A. " The first week in September."

Q. " In Glasgow? "

A. " Yes, sir."

Q. " By appointment? "

A. " Yes."

Q. " When next? "

A. " I have not met him since."

Q. " And you say he only called once at the country place? "

A. " Once, sir."

Q. " In your Glasgow deposition you say: ' He visited me at Girvan and was entertained at tea with me on Saturday night, and at dinner on Sunday with Miss Gilchrist and me.' "

A. " Yes, sir."

Q. " Then you did see him more than once in the country."

A. " Once."

He read the extract again as above.

Q. " Was that true? "

A. " Yes."

Q. " Then you invited this man to tea at Miss Gilchrist's summer house? "

A. " Yes."

Q. " On Saturday night? "

A. " Yes."

Q. " And on Sunday night? "

A. " He wasn't there."

Q. " On Sunday you invited him there to dinner with Miss Gilchrist and yourself, didn't you? "

A. " Yes, sir. I didn't invite him."

Q. " Who invited him."

A. " Miss Gilchrist."

Q. "Had you introduced him?"

A. "Yes, sir."

Q. "He was your friend, wasn't he?"

A. "Yes, sir."

Q. "She knew nothing about him?"

A. "No."

Q. "She took him to the house on your recommendation?"

A. "Yes."

Q. "Did she wear her diamonds at this dinner party?"

A. "I don't remember."

Q. "You told him that she was a rich woman?"

A. "Yes."

Q. "Did you tell him that she had a great many jewels?"

A. "Yes."

Q. "Have your suspicions ever turned towards this man?"

A. "Never."

Q. "Do you know of any other man who would be as familiar with those premises, the wealth of the old lady, her jewelry, and the way to get into the premises as that man?"

A. "No, sir."

Q. "Was the man you met in the hall-way this man?"

A. "No, sir."

This is a condensation of a very interesting and searching piece of the cross-examination which reveals several things. One is Lambie's qualities as a witness. Another is the very curious picture of the old lady, the bookmaker and the servant-maid all sitting at dinner together. The last and most important is the fact, that a knowledge of the jewels had got out. Against the man himself there is no possible allegation. The matter was looked into by the police, and their conclusions were absolute, and were shared by those responsible for the defence. But is it to be believed that during the months which elapsed between this man acquiring this curious knowledge, and the actual crime, never once chanced to repeat to any friend, who in turn repeated it to another, the strange story of the lonely old woman and her hoard? This he would do in full innocence. It was a most natural thing to do. But, for almost the first

time in the case we seem to catch some
glimpse of the relation between possible cause
and effect, some connection between the dead
woman on one side, and outsiders on the other
who had the means of knowing something of
her remarkable situation.

There is just one other piece of Lambie's
cross-examination, this time from the Edinburgh trial, which I would desire to quote.
It did not appear in America, just as the
American extract already given did not appear in Edinburgh. For the first time they
come out together:

Q. "Did Miss Gilchrist use to have a
dog?"

A. "Yes, an Irish terrier."

Q. "What happened to it?"

A. "It got poisoned."

Q. "When was it poisoned?"

A. "I think on the 7th or 8th of September."

Q. "Was that thought to be done by some
one?"

A. "I did not think it, for I thought it
might have eaten something, but Miss Gil-

christ thought it was poisoned by some one."

Q. "To kill the watch-dog — was that the idea?"

A. "She did not say."

The reader should be reminded that Slater did not arrive in Glasgow until the end of October of that year. His previous residences in the town were as far back as 1901 and 1905. If the dog were indeed poisoned in anticipation of the crime, he, at least, could have had nothing to do with it.

There is one other piece of evidence which may, or may not have been of importance. It is that of Miss Brown, the schoolmistress. This lady was in court, but seems to have been called by neither side for the reason that her evidence was helpful to neither the prosecution nor the defence. She deposed that on the night of the murder, about ten minutes past seven, she saw two men running away from the scene. One of these men closely corresponded to the original description of the murderer before it was modified by Barrowman. This one was of medium build, dark hair and clean shaven, with three-quarter length grey overcoat, dark tweed cap, and both hands in his pockets. Here we have the actual assassin described to the life, and had Miss Brown declared that this man was the prisoner, she would have been a formidable addition to the witnesses for prosecution. Miss Brown, however identified Oscar Slater (after the usual absurd fashion of such identifications) as the second man, whom she describes, as of "Dark glossy hair, navy blue overcoat with velvet collar, dark trousers, black boots, something in his hand which seemed clumsier than a walking stick." One would imagine that this object in his hand would naturally be his hat, since she describes the man as bare-headed. All that can be said of this incident is that if the second man was Slater, then he certainly was not the actual murderer whose dress corresponds closely to the first, and in no particular to the second. To the Northern eye, all swarthy foreigners bear a resemblance, and that there was a swarthy man, whether foreign or not, concerned in this affair would seem to be beyond question. That there

78

should have been two confederates, one of whom had planned the crime while the other carried it out, is a perfectly feasible supposition. Miss Brown's story does not necessarily contradict that of Barrowman, as one would imagine that the second man would join the murderer at some little distance from the scene of the crime. However, as there was no cross-examination upon the story, it is difficult to know what weight to attach to it.

Let me say in conclusion that I have had no desire in anything said in this argument, to hurt the feelings or usurp the functions of anyone, whether of the police or the criminal court, who had to do with the case. It is difficult to discuss matters from a detached point of view without giving offence. I am well aware that it is easier to theorise at a distance than to work a case out in practice whether as detective or as counsel. I leave the matter now with the hope that, even after many days, some sudden flash may be sent which will throw a light upon as brutal and callous a crime as has ever been recorded in those black annals in which the criminologist finds the materials for his study. Meanwhile it is on the conscience of the authorities, and in the last resort on that of the community that this verdict obtained under the circumstances which I have indicated, shall now be reconsidered.

Arthur Conan Doyle.

Windlesham,
   Crowborough.

COPY OF MEMORIAL
FOR REPRIEVE

UNTO THE RIGHT HONOURABLE LORD PENTLAND, HIS MAJESTY'S SECRETARY OF STATE FOR SCOTLAND

MEMORIAL

ON BEHALF OF

OSCAR SLATER

THIS Memorial is humbly presented on behalf of Oscar Slater presently a Prisoner in the Prison of Glasgow, who was, in the High Court of Justiciary at Edinburgh, on Thursday, the sixth day of May, Nineteen hundred and nine, found guilty of the charge of murdering Miss Marion Gilchrist in her house in West Princes Street, Glasgow, and sentenced to death. The Prisoner is a Jew, and was born in Germany. He is 37 years of age.

The Jury returned a verdict of "Guilty" by a majority of nine to six, and the legal advisers of the condemned man hold a very strong opinion that the verdict of the majority of the Jury was not in accordance with the evidence led, and that this evidence was quite insufficient to identify the Prisoner with the murderer, and so to establish the Prisoner's guilt. This view, they believe, is shared by the general public of all classes in Scotland, and by the Glasgow press (vide leading article in The Glasgow Herald of 7th May, 1909, sent herewith).

Your Memorialist has endeavoured in this paper to deal with the matter as briefly and with as little argument as possible; but in view of the fact that the trial of the Prisoner occupied four days, it is inevitable that the Memorial should extend to some length.

It is common ground that the late Miss Gilchrist, a lady of about 82 years of age, resided alone with her domestic servant, Nellie Lambie, a girl of about 21 years of age.

According to the evidence of Lambie, the latter left Miss Gilchrist alone in the house at seven o'clock on the evening of 21st December, 1908, and went to purchase an evening paper. Lambie deponed that she securely shut the house door behind her, and also the door at the close, or street entry; that she was only absent about ten minutes; that on returning about ten minutes past seven o'clock she found the close door open; that upon ascending the stair she found Mr. Adams, a gentleman who resides in the flat below, standing at Miss Gilchrist's house door; that Adams informed her that he had gone up to Miss Gilchrist's door because he had heard knocking on the floor of Miss Gilchrist's house, and had rung the bell, but that he could obtain no admittance; that the lobby was lighted by one gas jet turned half up, but giving a good light; that Lambie thereupon opened the house door with her keys; that upon the door being opened a man came through the lobby or hall of Miss Gilchrist's house, passed Lambie and Adams, went downstairs, and disappeared; and that, upon Lambie and Adams entering the house, they found Miss Gilchrist lying on the dining-room floor dead, her head having been smashed.

Upon the Wednesday following the murder (23rd December, 1908), the Glasgow Police were informed by a message girl named Mary Barrowman (about 15 years of age), that she had seen a man wearing a Donegal hat and a light coat running out of the close which leads from the street to Miss Gilchrist's house shortly after seven o'clock on the night of the murder; that the man passed her, running at top speed; that she noticed that he was dark, and clean shaven, and that his nose was twisted towards the right side. The servant Lambie had also informed the Police that a gold cresent brooch, set in diamonds, had disappeared from Miss Gilchrist's house on the night of the murder, and that this was all of Miss Gilchrist's property that she missed. These statements were published in the Glasgow newspapers on Friday, 25th December, 1908, and following upon this the witness Allan Maclean, a member of a club to which Slater belonged, informed the Police that Slater's appearance somewhat corresponded with the description advertised, and that he had been trying to sell a pawn ticket for a diamond brooch. Following up this clue, the Police went to Slater's house at 69, St. George's Road, Glasgow, on the night of Friday, 25th December, and learned that he and Miss Andrée Antoine, with whom he had been cohabiting, had left Glasgow that night with their belongings. The Police thereafter ascertained that Slater had sailed on the " Lusitania " for New York from Liverpool on Saturday, 26th December, and cabled to the Authorities at New York to detain and search him on his arrival. This was done, and the pawn ticket, which he had been trying to sell, was found upon him, but turned out to be a pawn ticket for a brooch which belonged to Miss Antoine, had never belonged to Miss Gilchrist, and had been pawned a considerable time before the murder. Proceedings, however, were instituted for Slater's extradition. The witnesses Lambie, Adams, and Barrowman gave evidence in America, purporting to identify him as the man seen leaving Miss Gilchrist's house, and Slater was (he states of his own consent) extradited, and brought back to Scotland for trial.

An advertisement was published by the Authorities in Glasgow offering a reward of £200 for information which would lead to the arrest of the murderer.

The only evidence against Slater, which might be called direct evidence, was the evidence of the persons who saw a man walk out of the lobby or hall in Miss Gilchrist's house on the night of the murder (Lambie and Adams), or leaving the close leading therefrom, or running along the street (Barrowman).

At the trials Lambie professed to identify Slater, as the man whom she had seen leaving the house, by the side of his face. It was put to her, however, and clearly proved, that when she gave evidence in New York in the extradition proceedings she stated in Court there that she did not see the man's face, and professed to identify him by his walk. When Slater's own coat, the one found in his luggage, was shown to her at the trial, she at once remarked, even before it was unrolled, that it was not like the coat the man in the lobby wore — it was the coat. It was obviously impossible that she knew it to be the same coat. Lord Guthrie referred to this in his charge to the jury as a typical example of the nature of her evidence. With regard to the positive nature of her evidence generally, it is interesting to note that her first answer in America, when asked if she saw the man, was, " One is very suspicious, if anything." She stated that, when she saw Slater in the Central Police Office at Glasgow, she recognised him in his "own coat." It was proved that he was not then wearing his own coat, but one with which he had been dressed for identification purposes.

The witness only saw the man who was leaving the house for a moment or two. Adams and she contradicted each other as to where she was when the man walked across the lobby. Adams deponed that she was by the lobby clock and walking towards the kitchen. If so, she must practically have had her back to the man. She says she was on the threshold of the door. In any event, her view was momentary.

The witness Adams, who deponed that he had a better view of the man in the house than Lambie, stated at the trial that he, standing at the threshold, saw the man's face as he approached, that their eyes met, and that the man walked slowly towards him, face to face, but Adams would not go further than to say that Slater resembled the man very much. He is superior to Lambie and Barrowman in years, education and intelligence. Your Memorialist begs to emphasise the fact that this witness had a much better view of the man than any of the other witnesses.

The witness Barrowman stated at the trial

that the man ran out of the close and rushed past her at top speed, brushing against her, and that he had his hat pulled well down over his forehead. The witness is a message girl, about 15 years of age. She also stated that the man had on brown boots, a Donegal hat, and a fawn coat, and that he was dark and clean shaven, and that his nose had a twist to the right. She professed to have noticed all these things as he rushed past her at top speed. At the trial this witness stated in cross-examination (1) that she was proceeding in the opposite direction from the man, to deliver a parcel, but that she turned and went some distance after him; that she thought he was probably going to catch a tram-car; but she could not explain why she should go out of her way to turn and follow a man running for a car in a busy city like Glasgow; and (2) that, although the girl Lambie and she had occupied the same cabin on the voyage to America, which lasted about twelve days, she had not once discussed the appearance of the man, and that no one had warned her not to do so. These two statements do not impress your Memorialist as bearing the stamp of truth. This girl started the description of the twisted nose. She is the only witness who refers to it. Her view of the man's face must necessarily have been momentary. Slater's nose cannot properly be described as "twisted to the right." It has a noticeable prominence in the centre. .

All of these three witnesses had, as has been said, only a momentary view of the man, and it was proved that before Barrowman professed to identify Slater in New York she was shown his photograph, and that both she and Lambie, before attempting to identify him in New York, saw him being brought into Court by a Court official, wearing a badge. In her New York evidence she first said, "He is something like the man I saw." At the trial she stated that he was the man. These facts very much reduce, if they do not altogether vitiate, the value of the evidence of these identifying witnesses.

Another witness, Mrs. Liddell, who is a married sister of the witness Adams, stated that, at five minutes to seven on the evening of the murder, she saw a dark, clean-shaven man leaning against a railing at the street entry to Miss Gilchrist's house, but that this man wore a heavy brown tweed coat and a brown cap. It is to be observed that Constable Neil, who passed the house at ten minutes to seven, saw no one there; and Lambie, who left the house promptly at seven, or, as she said in America, "perhaps a few minutes before seven," saw no one there. Further, Mrs. Liddell did not observe where the man went to; according to her he merely glided away; and although she was in Miss Gilchrist's house that night and saw the body, and would naturally be greatly concerned over the murder, she did not recollect having seen this man until the Wednesday after the murder. Even taking her evidence as absolutely true and reliable, it provides an excellent object-lesson on the difficulty and responsibility of convicting on such evidence as this, because the man she saw was obviously dressed differently from the man seen by the other three witnesses. Her evidence does not, to any appreciable extent, further the case against Slater, as she stated that she thought this man was Slater, but admitted that she might be in error.

The other witness is a girl named Annie Armour, a ticket clerk in the Subway Station at Kelvinbridge, who says that between 7.30 and 8 that evening a man, whom she identified as Slater, rushed past her office without waiting for a ticket, and seemed excited. Lord Guthrie in his charge to the jury did not refer to this witness, and your Memorialist thinks advisedly. The mere question of time is sufficient to render her evidence valueless. She is sure the incident did not happen before 7.30. According to the other witnesses, the murderer must have run from the house by at least 7.15. It was proved that it would only take a man five or six minutes to run from the scene of the tragedy to this station, either by the most direct route or by the route which Barrowman's evidence suggests he took. Then it is impossible to suppose that she could get anything like a good view, even of the side face, of a man who rushed past her in the way she described.

All the witnesses who saw the man on the night of the murder (Monday) say that he was clean shaven. It was proved that on the next day or two after the murder Slater had a short, black, stubbly moustache.

These were the only witnesses called by the Crown to identify Slater with the murderer. Further circumstantial evidence, however, was led by the Crown to show that, on occasions before the day of the murder, Slater had been seen standing in or walking up and down West Princes Street — Mrs. M'Haffie, her daughters and niece, Campbell, Cunningham, Bryson, Nairn, and O'Brien and Walker (two policemen). It may be noted that Slater's house was situated about three minutes' walk from West Princes Street.

These witnesses did not all agree in their evidence. Some said that Slater was the man they had seen; others, equally or perhaps better able to judge, only said that he was very like him. The Memorialist does not propose in this paper to deal at length with this part of the evidence, except to point out that two witnesses (Nairn and Bryson) say they saw Slater in West Princes Street on the Sunday evening previous to the murder. Against this there is the evidence that Slater on this day, as usual, spent all Sunday (day and evening) in his house. Three witnesses from Paris, London, and Dublin spoke to this. Coming from different places, they had no chance to concoct a story.

At Slater's trial it was suggested that there were various circumstances tending to create an atmosphere of suspicion around him; but it is submitted that all these were capable of explanation, and in no way pointing to Slater's guilt as a murderer. Slater had written to Cameron that he could prove where he was on the evening of the murder " by five people." When this letter was written, he thought that the date of the murder was the Tuesday, the 22nd.

The evidence of his witnesses was to the effect that on the evening of the murder he was in a billiard room until 6.30 p. m., after which he went home for dinner.

It was shown that Slater dealt in diamonds. There was, however, no evidence of any dishonest dealing of any kind. The brooch said to have been missing from Miss Gilchrist's house has not been traced. There was no evidence of any kind led to show that Slater ever knew, or even heard of, Miss Gilchrist or her house, and the Memorialist would emphasise the fact that it was the missing brooch that put the Police on the track of Slater.

With reference to Slater's departure for America on 25th December, 1908, it was proved that he had formed the intention, some weeks before the murder, of going to America. Cameron, Rattman, and Aumann proved this. Slater had, in fact, tried to get the last named to take over his flat. The letter from Jacobs, of 28th December, and the card bearing the words " address till 30th December," produced by the Crown, also corroborate the evidence of this intention of leaving, which is further corroborated by the evidence of Nichols, the barber, a Crown witness.

On the morning of 21st December, 1908, Slater received two letters — one from London, stating that his wife was demanding his address, and the other from San Francisco, asking him to come over. These were spoken to by Schmalz, his servant girl, and Miss Antoine. Further corroboration of his intention to leave is (1) on the morning of 21st December he raised a further £30 from Mr. Liddell, pawnbroker, on his brooch, and on the same day tried to sell the ticket; (2) he wrote to the Post Office for payment of the money at his credit; (3) he wired to Dent, London, to send on his watch, which was being repaired, immediately; (4) on the Monday morning he gave notice to the servant girl that she would not be required after the following Saturday (these events all happened before the murder); (5) on the Tuesday morning he redeemed a pair of binoculars from another pawnbroker whose assistant, Kempton, proved this, and who stated that he was in no way excited; (6) on the 23rd and 24th December he made inquiries at Cook's Shipping Offices regarding berths, and betrayed no signs of any excitement; on the 23rd he was, in the evening, in Johnston's billiard room, which he used to frequent; and on the 24th he spent the afternoon about Glasgow with his friend Cameron, who gave evidence; (7) on Friday morning a Mrs. Freedman and her sister arrived from London to take over his flat, so that he and Miss Antoine left on Friday night.

A rumour got abroad at the time to the effect that he booked to London and left the train at Liverpool. This rumour was published in the various newspapers, to Slater's great prejudice, but nothing of the kind was proved at the trial. The Police were evidently misled by the fact that he went by a London train, but it was proved that there were two carriages in that train for Liverpool, and also that Slater's luggage, consisting of nine boxes, was labelled to Liverpool. The Porter who labelled the luggage was called, and stated that Slater told him that he was going to Liverpool, and entered a Liverpool carriage.

The point was also raised against Slater that he used various aliases. He had been staying apart from his wife for about four years, during which time he cohabited with Miss Antoine. She stated that Slater's wife was a drunken woman, and caused him a deal of trouble. At one time he adopted the name of "George," and when he came to Glasgow on the last occasion he took the name of "Anderson." On the voyage to America he took the name of Otto Sando, because his luggage was labelled O. S. At times he called himself a dentist. There was no evidence that he really was a dentist. Miss Antoine explained that he adopted the title of dentist, as he required a designation of some sort, although he was a gambler. A great deal was published in the newspapers about a hammer that had been found in one of his boxes. This turned out to be an ordinary small domestic nail hammer, purchased on a card containing several other tools, the lot costing only 2s. 6d. He, of course, took the hammer to America with him with all the rest of his belongings.

Nothing incriminating was found in any of his boxes.

No evidence whatever was led to show how the murderer gained access to the house.

It will be conceded that identification evidence, especially in a serious charge of this kind, must be examined very carefully, and should have little weight attached to it, unless it is very clear.

To sum up, the only real evidence in the case is that of those who saw a man running away on the night of the murder; and, as has been pointed out, these witnesses had only a momentary glance at him. Adams does not positively identify the prisoner as the man. He says he closely resembles him.

Lambie's New York evidence has already been referred to, and her evidence at the trial cannot be reconciled with it.

. Lambie and Barrowman both saw him in custody before trying to identify him in New York, and the latter, before identifying him, was shown his photograph.

All the other identifying witnesses called to give evidence as to his having been seen in the vicinity on days previous to the murder were taken down to the Ceneral Police Office when Slater returned from America to identify him. They were shown into one room together, and then separately taken into a room in the Police

Office, where Slater was amongst about a dozen men, none of whom were like him. (Cunningham says she could see that the other men were policemen in plain clothes.) All these witnesses knew that Slater had arrived from America, and was in the room. They had all read his description in the newspapers, or had seen his photograph. They all, therefore, looked for, and had no difficulty in pointing out, a dark, foreign-looking man, with a somewhat peculiarly shaped nose. It is submitted that this is not identification evidence in the proper sense at all. Had these people been able to pick out, as their man, from amongst several others, a man whose description they only knew from what they had previously seen of him, unassisted by description, and unassisted by a photograph, the value of their evidence would have been entirely different.

Some Crown witnesses identified him as the man they had seen and talked to (Shipping Clerk, Porter, &c.), but they, of course, were able to do so. None of the identifying witnesses had ever spoken to him.

Identification evidence is a class of evidence which the law distrusts. The most famous authority is the case of Adolf Beck. Beck was, in 1896, sentenced to seven years' penal servitude, on the evidence of ten women, who swore positively that he was a man whom they had each met on two occasions, and spent some time with in their own houses, and who had defrauded them, and on the evidence of two policemen, who swore positively that Beck was the man who had been previously convicted of similar crimes, taken along with certain circumstantial evidence — that he was known to frequent a hotel on the notepaper of which one of the women had received a letter. Again, in 1904, Beck was convicted of similar crimes on similar evidence. It was subsequently demonstrated that Beck committed none of the crimes, but that a man bearing a general similarity to him was the criminal.

In the report issued by the Commission appointed to investigate the matter, consisting of Lord Collins, Sir Spencer Walpole, and Sir John Edge, the following passage occurs: — " Evidence of identity, upon personal impression, however bona fide, is of all classes of evidence the least to be relied upon, and, unless supported by other evidence, an unsafe basis for the verdict of a Jury."

Now, the evidence in the Beck case was infinitely more overwhelming and consistent than in this case; and the report in the Beck case, and the report on which it followed, make it clear that on the evidence in this case the Jury had no right to bring in a verdict of " Guilty."

THE CASE OF OSCAR SLATER

A good deal was said by the learned Lord Advocate to the Jury about Slater's immoral character. It was not disputed that he was a gambler. It was also admitted that he had cohabited for about four years with Madame Antoine, who was of doubtful virtue, and who gave evidence. Yet the learned Lord Advocate addressed the Jury to the effect that the prisoner " had followed a life which descended to the very depth of human degradation, for, by the universal judgment of mankind, the man who lived upon the proceeds of prostitution has sunk to the lowest depth, and all moral sense in him had been destroyed." This he cited as proof of the disappearance of an obstacle which had previously been in his way, viz: — Whether it was conceivable that such a man as Slater could commit such an inhumanly brutal crime. The only evidence on that point was that of Cameron, Slater's friend, who, in cross-examination, said he had heard that Slater lived on the earnings of prostitution, but who did not say he knew. The Jury were distinctly told by the Lord Advocate, and by the prisoner's Counsel, and by the Judge, to banish from their minds anything they had heard regarding the man's character; but they had previously heard all about it, and the Memorialist feels strongly that they were evidently unable to do so.

Public feeling is also very strong on the point that the question of Slater's character should never have been brought before the Jury.

The Memorialist thinks it is only fair to prisoner to point out that he was all along anxious to give evidence on his own behalf. He was advised by his Counsel not to do so, but not from any knowledge of guilt. He had undergone the strain of a four days' trial. He speaks rather broken English — although quite intelligibly — with a foreign accent, and he had been in custody since January.

Apart from what has been set forth above, your Memorialist begs to draw attention to the fact that on the Crown list of witnesses is the name of a witness, Miss Agnes Brown (No. 46). This lady is 30 years of age, and a very intelligent school teacher. Your Memorialist is informed that she told the Police and Procurator-Fiscal that on the night of the murder, about ten minutes past seven o'clock, two men in company rushed along West Princes Street from the direction of Miss Gilchrist's house, and passed close to her at the corner of West Princes Street and West Cumberland Street; that one of them was dressed in a blue Melton coat with a dark velvet collar, black boots, and without a hat; that both men ran past the opening of West Cumberland Street, straight on along West Princes

Street, crossed West Princes Street, and ran down Rupert Street, a street further west, and opening off the opposite side of West Princes Street. Your Memorialist understands that, in the identification proceedings before referred to, this witness pointed out Slater as the man in the Melton coat, as she thought. This witness's evidence is thus in sharp contradiction on material points to that of the message girl Barrowman (who had only a momentary glance at the man), but upon whose evidence so much weight has evidently been laid, and who says that Slater was dressed in a light coat, a Donegal hat, and brown boots, was alone, and ran down West Cumberland Street.

Your Memorialist respectfully submits that this illustrates the danger of convicting a man upon the kind of evidence given in this case. Miss Brown was in attendance at the trial, but was not called as a witness. Even on the evidence led, the votes of two more jurymen in his favour would have liberated the prisoner. In England the probability is that a conviction would never have been obtained.

Your Memorialist is authorised to state that Slater's Counsel agree that the evidence did not justify the conviction.

Your Memorialist, who has all along acted as Slater's Solicitor since he was brought back from

THE CASE OF OSCAR SLATER

America after the Extradition Proceedings, and who has had very many interviews with Slater, begs respectfully to state his absolute belief in Slater's innocence.

May it therefore please the Right Honourable the Secretary of State for Scotland to take this Memorial into his most favourable consideration, and thereafter to advise his Most Gracious Majesty to exercise his royal prerogative to the effect of commuting the sentence passed upon the prisoner, or to do otherwise as in the circumstances may seem just.

And your Memorialist will ever pray.

EWING SPIERS,
190 West George Street, Glasgow,
Oscar Slater's Solicitor.

Dated this seventeenth day of May, One thousand nine hundred and nine.

[Wide World Photo.]

GETS $30,000. Oscar Slater paid by British government for wrongful conviction of murder.

CLEAR SLATER AFTER 20 YEARS

International News Ser v s Cable

EDINBURGH, Scotland, July 20.
—One of the most sensational murder cases in British history was a closed incident today when Scottish courts quashed the conviction of Oscar Slater, released last November after serving almost 18 years for killing aged Miss Marion Gilchrist at Glasgow. The Slater case was compared by some to the Sacco-Vanzetti case. Although released from the penitentiary, the Slater conviction continued to stand until today.

Slater was arrested in New York in 1908, as he left the liner Lusitania. He waived extradition and was convicted largely by three witnesses, one a young woman, Helen Lambie, who subsequently migrated to the United States and married.

Slater was sentenced to death, but sentence was commuted to life imprisonment. After his release a movement was started to have the conviction annulled. Sir Arthur Conan Doyle interested himself in Slater's behalf.

CPSIA information can be obtained at www.ICGtesting.com
Printed in the USA
LVOW111629050812

293000LV00012BA/102/P